Boom Town Reflections

Volume – 1

Love and the Rocky Road to Maturity

Mark A. Gregg

This book is dedicated to Vangie, the most amazing woman in the world. She is my wife, soulmate, and best friend. We have lived every moment of this incredible journey together. No one knows her fierce tenacity and genuine tenderness like I do.

Copyright © 2024 by Mark A. Gregg
All rights reserved.

Table Of Contents

~1~ The Beginning 1

~2~ The Racing Bug 7

~3~ Everyone Goes To See 28

~4~ The Love Of My Life 38

~5~ Marriage At Sixteen? 52

~6~ The Wedding And The Governor 68

~7~William Hurlemann President, Wurlitzer Organ Company 79

~1~
THE BEGINNING

1956 was a memorable year for America. Dwight David "Ike" Eisenhower served as the 34th President of the United States. Chevrolet introduced two four-barrel carburetors as a performance option for its 265 Cubic Inch small block V-8 engine, known as the turbo-fire V-8. This engine powered the Chevrolet Bel Air, one of the most iconic cars in American history.

I made my involuntary debut in Loveland, Colorado, in December 1956, three years into Ike's presidency. Though my memories of the 1950s are limited, I believe America was an amazing place to live. The post-war economy was booming, and families across the country were experiencing prosperity like never before.

You should note that I am not very bright (this memoir is a living proof), but I have an excellent memory. Whether this is a blessing, or a curse remains to be seen; it can go either way.

In 1956, my parents were in their late 20s and already seasoned in the art of child-rearing. They blessed me with three older brothers, born about nine months and 15 minutes apart: Wylie in 1949, Mike in 1950, and Larry in 1951.

All four of us boys were born in Colorado. Dad worked for the United States Bureau of Reclamation as a hydroelectric power plant operator near Green Mountain, and later at the Flatiron hydroelectric plant in Loveland. He was passionate about the utility industry and steadily rose through the ranks, eventually retiring as the Chief Dispatcher in the Western Area Power Administration (WAPA) in 1982.

While my Dad was primarily working with hydroelectric plants, the 1950's saw a building boom of large, coal-fired power stations. Inexpensive electricity was crucial for maintaining economic growth, which brought forth the construction of larger and more efficient coal-firedplants.

As a fuel, coal was inexpensive, abundant, and was the energy king in spite of its drawbacks. The fossil energy sector's growth in the 60's, 70's and 80's put a substantial number of people with barely a high school diploma firmly into the economic middle class. I can testify that some of these diploma recipients were thoroughly undeserved after working with them through the years. Of course, *many of them undoubtedly said the same of me.*

Not long after I was born, Dad moved into a power operations dispatcher position within the Bureau of Reclamation. This required us to move from the Colorado mountains to Watertown, South Dakota. Watertown, the seat of Codington County, was a modest, aging community of about 14,000 people in eastern South Dakota, near the Minnesota border.

It was during my kindergarten year that Dad took me to the small, municipal, steam power plant in Watertown. For a totally unknown reason, I was instantly and irreversibly captivated by the deafening noise, sweltering heat, and mechanical rhythm experienced in that fascinating place. This visit ignited a lifelong passion for these mechanical dinosaurs, and the power industry in general. This passion ballooned as I grew older and spent time around my Dad, and his involvement in the power industry. It became the basis of all my future endeavors.

Watertown saw two more additions to the Gregg family: Patricia in 1960 and Barbara in 1962, bringing our total to six children. It is still surprising to me that there were six children due to my Dad's dislike of babies, adolescents, teenagers, and young adults. Dad's favorite child was anyone over 21 *not related to him.* In retrospect, despite his issues with kids, he did a decent job raising us.

In 1963, Mom and Dad announced we were moving back to Colorado. Dad accepted a power operations dispatcher job with the Bureau of Reclamation at a new dispatch center built in Montrose, Colorado. The Bureau ofReclamation was building three large dams on the Gunnison River and opened a new power dispatching center in Montrose to control the electrical generation fromthese three behemoths.

Blue Mesa, Morrow Point, and Crystal dams were the cornerstone of the Curecanti project in western Colorado. The construction of these three, massive dams took over 15 years with Blue Mesa being the single largest body of water in Colorado. They were built for both power generation andwater conservation purposes.

Montrose is nestled in the Uncompahgre Valley near the majestic San Juan Mountains. I grew up there, taking the staggering beauty of the area for granted untiladulthood.

In the early summer of 1964, the Gregg family, consisting of Mom, Dad, the half-dozen Gregg kids, and a big yellow dog named King, were crammed into a two-tone pink and white 1958 Pontiac station wagon, embarking on the grueling journey to Montrose, Colorado. Automotive air conditioning was rare back then, making the car unbearably hot, smelly, and uncomfortable.

Dad attempted to turn the move to Colorado into a bit of a vacation by stopping at the Black Hills and the Badlands of South Dakota. We visited several tourist traps in the Black Hills, including the mighty and majestic Mount Rushmore, which fascinated me for a fleeting few minutes. As a focus-impaired seven-year-old, stone faces quickly lost their charm. Mostly, I remember the discomfort of the hot, noisy, smelly car that felt like an oven on wheels. We traveled with the windows wide open, force-ventilating the pink and white beast as it carried us to the mysterious land of Colorado.

After moving to Montrose and starting 2nd grade, I skillfully developed a knack for barely passing school classes. I carefully managed to scrape by with D's. The only class I ever flunked was in High School. It was Mr. Strakbein's biology class. He failed me outright. Oddly, I believe I knew as much or more than my peers in that class; he was just being ornery because he knew I wasn't paying attention. I had to repeat his class, but I passed it with a B the second time—certainly the highest grade I ever earned in High School.

From an educational standpoint, the three best things Dad did for me were teaching me to work on engines, buying me a Heathkit® electronics builder, and taking me to the Montrose dispatch center at the Bureau of Reclamation during his afternoon shifts.

A Heathkit® electronics builder (for those who may notknow) was a 15" x 15" circuit board with resistors, capacitors, transistors, and other electronic components mounted on it. Each component could be connected using the supplied wires to complete a circuit. You could build various simple electric circuits, including a radio. I learneda tremendous amount from the exercises in this kit.

The trips to the dispatch center were a bit controversial. My Mom would drop me off with his dinner around 5:00 or6:00 in the evening during his afternoon shifts. I would spend the entire evening with him until he went home at midnight. He guided me through high-voltage, electrical switching and various other control operations. The dispatch center managed the electrical distribution grid in this part of Colorado and controlled the power plants at the Curecanti Project dams.

Dad would carefully direct me as I performed control changes and other functions. He would show me how to do something once, and then let me do it myself. If I didn't remember exactly how it was done, he would become irate,yelling at me for almost causing a catastrophic grid failure or triggering one of many other potential disasters. It was thrilling and disabling all at the same time.

There were always two dispatchers on shift. I suspect Dad's partner complained about having a 12/13-year-old kid handling controls that could disrupt the power grid. After several non-consecutive nights working with Dad, someone higher up put a stop to it. He even showed me the memo prohibiting "children under the age of 18 years" from being in the dispatch and control area. It was unfortunate, as I learned a great deal about the power grid, power plants, and dams during those visits. Each visit exponentially increased my desire to work in the power industry.

I cannot overstate how crucial these experiences were to my development. Despite his flaws, Dad was spot-on in exposing me to these vital areas of knowledge. They formed a lasting foundation for my future.

Dad was always furious—there's no other word for it—when report cards came out, and I presented him with straight D's. He offered money and other incentives to improve my grades, but nothing ever worked. I have many regrets about not trying harder in school. I often think that if I had the chance to do it over, I would apply myself and get better grades. Probably not. Sometimes, I think we are who we are, no matter how much we try to fool ourselves.

~2~
THE RACING BUG

I finished my freshman year in High School with the expected 'D' average in all subjects, and I was perfectly content with my performance. A 'D' says, "Move on," while an 'F' means, "Do it over." I was comfortable with a 'D' average. It allowed me to be lazy with minimal consequences.

Dad blamed my poor academic performance on my lack of involvement in high school sports which always puzzled me. I couldn't see the connection between sports and my grades. Mom thought it was because I didn't have any friends. Again, I didn't understand the connection. However, that was about to change.

I met Ron Wamsley at the end of our freshman year. Ron was a loner. His parents were divorced, and he and his two sisters lived with their mother, who was, at best, promiscuous. Combined with an abusive father, this had a significant impact on him. They divorced because his dad had a psychotic temper and was physically abusive.

In retrospect, Ron inherited his father's temper and issues. Despite this, we became inseparable friends. Ron was dark and moody but very athletic, excelling on the wrestling team at school. Most girls, including my sisters thought he was a good-looking "hunk." He worked hard to maintain his chiseled physique and talked incessantly about wrestling. I had no interest in wrestling or sports in general.

Our friendship was based on a shared bond; *alcohol*. We both liked to drink.

Academically, neither of us did very well. Ron didbetter than I did because he needed to maintain his sports eligibility. I didn't want to play sports, so that wasn't an issue for me. It wasn't that I hated watching sports, but I was not athletically inclined and did not have an ounce of interest in any sport I participated.

Dad and I had routine, sometimes even explosive arguments about my grades in school. I would always argue that I was learning more than the other students because I was reading and retaining what I read. While that wasn't entirely true, he wanted to believe it. I did tend to be a trivia king, spouting a lot of basically useless information.

Ron got his driver's license when I was 15. His dad gave him their old 1963 Oldsmobile sedan. It was a massive, faded-blue land yacht that measured gas mileage in gallons per mile and not miles per gallon. However, it became the ultimate party vehicle.

We were in that Oldsmobile every spare moment, usually trying to hustle someone to buy beer for us. It's still amazing to think about how many people of legal age agreed to buy beer for us. I don't recall ever failing to get itdone. I still contemplate how stupid these people were to buy us beer. Besides being illegal, what good did they think would come from it?

During our sophomore year Ron and I figured out how to perfectly replicate our parents' signatures on themandatory excuse forms school absences. We were careful never to visit the attendance office at the same time and always acted sick when getting our excuse slips. This allowed us to miss school any day we wanted.

We missed over 30 days during our sophomore year. You might wonder what we did on these days. Drinking? Sometimes. But usually we drove to Grand Junction, 60 miles away, to eat at Taco Bell. Montrose didn't have a Taco Bell in the early '70s. Grand Junction did, and it was our slice of heaven. We always ordered the same thing; red burritos with no onions. We'd sit in the car, savor ourburritos, and listen to KEXO, the local rock radio station. We left Grand Junction early to avoid being seen, returningaround the time school let out in Montrose.

Once, we went too far. After a group of loud college students arrived at Taco Bell after us, we recklessly disabled their car by removing the spark plug wires and distributor cap. We sped away in the Oldsmobile, tires squealing, narrowly avoiding a collision with another car as we hit North Avenue and headed home. Fortunately, they never caught us.

This incident had unintended consequences. The college students undoubtably saw the Oldsmobile and knew we were the culprits that disabled their car. This fear forour lives kept us from returning to Grand Junction for many weeks, which somehow led to me staying in school just enough to pass into my junior year at Montrose High School. *Funny how things like this work out.*

In December 1972, I achieved a significant milestone. I received my driver's license and started working for Dwayne Morris at the Pioneer 66 filling station on South Townsend Avenue in Montrose. The station specialized in heavy mechanical work and radiator repair. Dwayne and his wife Clarabelle owned the station. Dwayne was often sick and cranky due to the chemicals he worked with while repairing radiators, and Clarabelle had her good and bad days. Mostly bad.

Dwayne put me to work overhauling engines, and doing carburetor, ignition, brake, and transmission work. Despite starting late in the year, I earned $374, a decent amount for working after school and weekends, considering the median yearly income for an adult male was $7,450.

In 1973, I made $1,547 working part-time. It was good money for a 16-year-old. However, my biggest problem was my alcohol consumption. Ron was complicit, drinking as much or more than I did. His psychotic temper made him a formidable presence, and I sometimes felt the brunt of his anger. His muscular physique and wrestling ability made him a force to reckon with.

Once, during one of our Taco Bell trips, I accidentally ordered green burritos instead of red while he sat in the car listening to a song he liked. When I returned to the car with the green burritos instead of red, Ron went into a rage, threw the burritos out the window, and drove like a complete maniac back to Montrose. His explosive wrath rattled me and I lost trust in him, despite being best friends.

Ron started using drugs about a year into our friendship, but I abstained. One night, while looking for someone to buy us beer, Ron's acquaintances began smoking pot in the car. I asked to be let out and I walked home. Seeing the effect of drugs on Ron only reinforced my decision to stay away from them. As Ron moved on to harder drugs and hallucinogens, his mood and bizarre temper darkened further.

Ron worked after school and Saturdays at the John Deere dealer, where the owner and his chief mechanic raced stock cars. We were so exhilarated by watching the races that we decided to get into racing ourselves.

We pooled our money to buy a used 1958 Ford sedan from the back-lot of Carrington Chevrolet. We were incredible negotiators. It was worth no more than $75.00, but we paid $150.00 for it. The car was dark green, dented, scratched, abused, and had high mileage, but it ran well. Since I had the tools and access to a welder, the old Ford went to my backyard for us to perform mechanical magic.

The first thing we did was remove the muffler. It had a 292 cubic inch V-8. In most circles, this was considered far more of a truck engine than a racing engine. However, with the muffler removed, *it sounded like a racing engine to us.*

We reversed the rear spring shackles, raising the rear of the car a bit. This was the exact opposite of what you should do for an oval track car. However, we just didn't know any better. The next step was to get a rule book for the local tracks and then begin the building process.

In 1973, just as now, building a dirt-track race car from scratch was costly. With both our incomes we might have completed it if we had any discipline at all. However, we still had to buy beer, gas, snacks, and keep our street cars running. I owned a 1964 Ford Fairlane, 2-door hardtop with a factory-installed high performance (K Code) 271 HP 289 Cubic Inch V-8. It ran quite well but was a money pit.

Ron's drug use was costing him increasingly more money as time passed.

The end result was inevitable... Dad hauled the 1958 Ford to the salvage yard in the fall of 1972. By then, we had only managed to remove the muffler and reverse the rear spring shackles. We never found the money or time to do anything more.

Raleigh Hale, an eccentric former employer, knew we were trying to build a race car. He knew of a practically track-ready car. The owner wanted out of racing due to the time and cost.

It was a 1959 Ford, and painted a flawless and exquisite John Deere Green from its previous sponsorship by the John Deere Implement company in Montrose. Raleigh said he would get us the car if we agreed to repaint it because he hated John Deere Green. What a shame. The only good thing about this car was the John Deere Green paint job!

When Raleigh offered the stock car, Ron was too absorbed in drugs and partying to care about racing. I accepted the stock car from Raleigh with the proviso that I repainted it. He even gave me some silver paint to cover the beautiful John Deere Green finish. *Wow!* What a disaster that was. I painted it in the backyard while the wind was at gale force.

I borrowed a compressed air sprayer and used a compressor that couldn't keep up, causing it to 'splutter' instead of spray. I ended up with a coat of silver stucco on the car. It was hilarious how bad this paint job was. I didn't even prep the surface. Within a few days, the silver stucco began peeling off revealing the John Deere Green underneath. However, even the custom stucco paint job was still substantially better than the actual car.

I painted the number 16 on the side of the car with red spray paint. This was my number. I was 16 years old and liked adding numbers together. 1 plus 6 was 7. Apparently, 7 was supposed to be a lucky number. Since no other car at the track had the number 16, I was in luck.

The first race in Montrose was the following weekend. I couldn't drive or test the car before my first race because I didn't have a trailer to haul it to the track. We had to tow it behind my dad's pickup with a tow bar, which was a screeching, convulsive spectacle.

The rear differential on the stock car was modified to be a "locker." This means both rear wheels are locked together and must turn at the same speed whether going straight or turning a corner. In a corner, the inside wheel must turn slower than the outside wheel, causing the wheels to fight and skid. This improves traction on a racetrack but causes the rear wheels to fight each other on any corner. Towing the car to the track on scorching hot pavement caused a teeth-grating squeal as the tires aggressively fought each other.

My first race at the Montrose track was a nerve- wracking ordeal, though I was too macho and driven by testosterone to show it. The steering gear on the car was so worn out that the steering wheel had over a ¾ turn of "play." I could spin the wheel nearly a full revolution before the front wheels responded. On Montrose's rough, dusty, high-banked dirt track, this made the car handle like it was being driven by a drunkard—it was all over the place.

At just 16 and with no prior experience driving a race car, this was my first time behind the wheel of one. The result was a spectacular display of exactly how NOT to race. Out of the five cars in my class, I left a gratuitous amount of silver paint on each, along with several light poles and barriers around the track and pit area. My indiscriminate banging into everything turned the race into a comedic spectacle for the spectators who managed to avoid my chaos.

Dad came to the races that day, having shown little interest in my life's pursuits up until then. After watching the heat race, semi-main, and main event, he examined the car and concluded it was a complete, uncompromised piece of junk. He also took the opportunity to explain that new drivers typically take almost two years to develop even mediocre peripheral vision, which might explain my difficulties on the track.

Thanks, Dad. I really needed to hear why I was so terrible at driving. However, something unexpected sparked in him. Having always had an interest in cars and trucks, he saw this as a chance to channel my energy into something productive and keep me out of trouble.

The next week before dragging the decaying, silver Ford to the track, Dad purchased an expensive tie-rod end for the front steering gear to get rid of some of the "slop" in the car's front-end. I couldn't believe it. He seemed to enjoy the involvement with the race car.

This was the only thing in my 16 years of life that Dad and I did together. Sure, he bought the Heath kit and taught me how engines worked, but this was obligatory in his mind. He wanted to teach me anything of value since I sucked so badly at school. The stock car was something completely different. We were doing something together as father and son, not a tense pairing of "disciplinarian and screw-up" as I normally felt with him.

When we got to the track, Raleigh Hale wanted to do a couple of "hot-laps" (practice laps) to see how the car "he got for me" performed. How could I refuse? Raleigh wasn'ta particularly good race car driver. However, he liked putting on a show. He was running the old, worn-out Ford right to the edge when the engine shelled-out on his third lap (blew-up).

I was thoroughly pissed. Smoke and steam blew out from the front fender wells as the stucco silver junker rolled to an abrupt stop on the edge of the pits. It appeared that my racing days started and ended with the prior week's racing. Little did I know…

Dad was not near as upset about the blown engine as I was. Raleigh was apologetic but hastily pointed out that the car was "a complete piece of junk." Funny how his opinion of the car "he got for me" changed so quickly. I was bummed and just wanted to go home. Dad chastised me and convinced me to go into the stands and watch the races. He disappeared as I walked across the track and into the stands. I knew he was still at the races because his pickup was the towing vehicle, and it was still sitting in the pits by the stock car.

Prior to Raleigh destroying my car's engine, I noticed a barrel-chested, Navajo Indian looking gentleman roll into the track parking lot. He had a stock car on a trailer behind his lumbering, brown 1969 Ford station wagon. It looked odd to see a stock car towed behind a station wagon. He had a sinister look to him. A cold shiver ran down my back the first time I saw him. He had a muscular build with a barrel chest, and long, jet-black hair combed straight back and down onto his shoulders. His eyes were malignant and piercing. If you were to personify Satan, it would be some form of his ugly mug. He was ominous and scary lookingto me.

His stock car was painted with flat black primer and had "for sale" sloppily painted with white paint on each side. We later learned he had recently moved his young family to Grand Junction from Utah. The stock car was a 1956 Ford that was professionally built and not just a junk heap like what I was racing now. He wanted $450.00 forthe car and trailer without an engine. I stared at the car sitting on the trailer and could only dream…

At the end of the semi-main event, when the cars for themain event were lining up, Dad came to the bottom of the rickety, poorly constructed stands and waved me over to him.

"Follow me." He said quickly. "I want to show you something." I followed him to the parking lot where the flat-black stock car sat on its trailer.

"Son, this is David George. He owns this car and the trailer." I shook his hand. Dad always taught me to have a good, solid, firm handshake. David's hand was akin tograbbing a cold, dead carp. A cold shiver ran down my back when I shook his hand.

David just stared at me and said in a deep, dead-pan voice, "How ya doin'?" Before I could answer him, Dad continued as if David was not standing right there.

"I'm trying to convince David to take $250.00 for the car and trailer." He turned and pointed to the trailer. "The trailer is junk. It is a single axle, home-built trailer without suspension, and the car doesn't have running gear." Dad then looked directly at David.

David scowled as he replied, "This car had a winning record at the track in Salt Lake City a few years back." His tone was ominous. "I built the damn trailer myself, and it made it *here* without any problems." Dad and he had a tense stare-down. David lost, breaking the silence first.

"$350.00. That's it. I ain't goin' no lower." He paused and looked in my direction. "I ain't even found a job here yet. I gotta live on this money for a while."

I was blown away that Dad was even discussing this. However, it made sense. Dad pushed Wylie, Mike, and Larry to be in sports. Football, wrestling, basketball… Didn't matter what it was, he pushed them. He was very vocal that participating in sports keeps kids out of trouble. Larry rebelled and refused to do sports, ending up with a police record (misdemeanors). In Dad's mind, this proved his theory. I tried going the sports route at Dad's insistence but was so awkwardly uncoordinated that he backed off his insistence that I participate.

Dad walked around the stock car one more time, poking his head into the fender wells and looking underneath. "Nope. Can't do $350.00. We must find an engine, transmission, and driveline. I will do $300.00, not a penny more." Dad then turned and looked at me.

"Let's go and watch the rest of the main event." Theroar of the cars on the track increased as we walked towards the track. It only took a minute before David George jogged up and aggressively grabbed Dad's shoulder.

He yelled over the roar of the cars on the track. "How soon could you have the cash?"

"Tomorrow," Dad replied.

"Done... $300.00." David looked fiercely angry as he said it. Looking at how incensed he was made me wonder why he took the deal if he was so upset about it. The fact that he had to live on the money from selling the car told me he had some serious issues.

The gravity of the situation finally sunk into my cranium. I almost couldn't believe it... ***Dad just bought me a race car!*** My mind was reeling as I thought about the missing engine transmission, and the work necessary to get this car back on the race track.

The next week was a blur. Dad enlisted a couple of sponsors. One of them was Del Weisner. Del's wife, Kay, was a guidance counselor at Montrose High School. I had dealt with her concerning my past truancy issues. I wasn't abig fan, even though she was a very thoughtful, sophisticated lady who treated me much better than I deserved.

Del owned a small trucking company, and he and my dad bought and sold several trucks together. Del used to race high-end drag cars (1/4-mile gassers) many years prior. He had a club-foot and walked with a noticeable limp from a near-deadly race car crash that ended his racing career 10 or 12 years earlier.

Dad went to work and quickly found a used 312 (cubic inch) engine and transmission for the stock car. The engine needed rebuilt, so he turned it over to me to put rings and bearings in it in preparation for the track. When I finished the overhaul a week or so later, we installed the powertrain in the car and took it to Del's shop for painting in his paint booth.

Del was a fantastic mechanic and an excellent automotive "body" man. He could repair dents and was an excellent painter. He loved racing and almost sacrificed his life for this love. Del and Kay never had children and were generally very private people. Getting involved with the stock car seemed to energize him.

Del painted it yellow with green trim simply because he had leftover paint that he had used on something else. We finished the paint job by painting the number "16" on each side in shadowed block lettering. It looked excellent! I couldn't wait to get it to the track. The engine sounded great, and I could drive it around Del's property. There was no room to *drive it, but I could* test the gears in his driveway.

My first race with the new # 16 was in Delta, Colorado. The track was north of town at the base of a large adobe hill. There were some makeshift bleachers, but most spectators would sit on the hill's steep slope using blankets and lawn chairs to watch the races. The DCRA (Delta County Racing Association) would densely pack the entire hill with racing fans looking for the thrill of competition and the excitement of the crashes. Stock car racing was a big deal in Delta in the mid-1970s.

On race day, each car and driver would do a time trial before the races started. The time trial consisted of a single car and driver making one complete lap around the track as fast as they could while being timed from the flag stand. The time to complete the lap determined where you lined- up during the races. I was so nervous that I had a bout with diarrhea prior to my time trial. I was only able to do a couple of hot-laps prior to the time trials, but I was impressed with the feel of the car.

My first night, I wasn't fast enough to make the main event, but I qualified for the semi-main event and associated heat races. Many of the banked oval dirt tracks of the day did not line up the cars the way NASCAR lines them up. In NASCAR, the faster a car completes a lap in the time trials, the closer to the front of the pack they get to start. The very fastest car in a NASCAR race gets awarded the coveted "pole position." This is the front row, inside position.

On the small, banked oval, dirt tracks the races are much shorter in duration than the NASCAR races. To keep the races interesting on the dirt tracks, the faster your time in the time trials, the further back you are slotted. The fastest car in the dirt track time trials is given the very back, outside position... Just the opposite of NASCAR. This way, the fastest cars must work past the slower cars to reach the front as quickly as possible to win the race.

This made the races incredibly fast-paced and harrowing, providing non-stop racing action. In theory, it was a great idea because it made the races interesting and, frankly, caused more wrecks. I am convinced, deep down, that wrecks in dirt track racing are usually one of the reasons some people even come to the races.

My first-time trial had me in the bottom half of the field. The top half of the field was in the "fast" heat races and the main event, while the bottom half of the field was in the "slow" heat races and the semi-main event. The biggest difference was the payout for 1st, 2nd, and 3rd place was higher in the main event. Obviously, the fastest cars were in the main event.

I did okay in my first couple of weeks of racing. The car and I were "learning" about each other. I was only 16 years old, and my inexperience as a driver was a liability *and* an asset. I didn't have any pre-learned driving habits, good or bad. I learned my visceral driving instincts on the track and not on the street. When other 16-year-old kids were learning to anticipate other drivers at intersections, I was learning to "drift" and anticipate what other race drivers were going to do as they were fighting for position and, ultimately, the win.

My lack of coordination in school sports did not seem to carry over into racing. Driving a race car on an oval track is more of a guttural "feel" in the core of your being than physical coordination. As I progressed each week, I felt the car and I were getting closer. I learned the difference between an under-steer, an over-steer, and a dry drift and a wet drift. My body instinctively reacted to the track and other cars without thought or planning.

I was learning continuously. I spun the car out many times in hot laps, time trials, and many times in actual races. I would be in one of the corners and drifting at a 45° angle, feeling like I was in total control, and the next thing I knew, the car's tail-end would come completely around, and I would be off the track or banging into another car. It was exhilarating, embarrassing, terrifying, and exasperating all rolled into one.

By the end of the season in 1973, I was winning some races. Ultimately, my faster time trials moved me into the "fast" heats and into the main event. I was getting a little quicker every single week. Once I moved up to the "big boys," as Dad called it, my winning streak was over. This is because I was now racing with substantially more experienced drivers and cars much faster than mine. I couldn't compete. I was just another one of the cars in the back of the pack at the end of a race.

In the last race of 1973, I rolled the car off the # 1 and # 2 banked corner at the Delta track. It was oddly exhilarating. I drifted too high in the corner and slid right over the top of the banked corner. The car rolled once or twice. I still don't know if I went over once or twice because it happened so fast. Remember, you are fully strapped into the car, and the dust and dirt on a dirt track opaque your vision. This is vastly multiplied when you roll. All the dust and dirt inside the car becomes airborne, and you are blinded. The centrifugal force of the car rolling confuses your senses. You are rapidly slammed in multiple directions losing all sense of location.

By the end of the season, the car was incredibly battered, and my rollover didn't help. I drove back into the pits with the car still marginally capable of being raced. However, it was the last race of the season. I was done, and the car needed a ton of work.

Dad was in the pits of every race and loved every moment of it. To be honest, I think he enjoyed racing more than I did. The Delta track had a mechanic's race during one of the weeks. Dad chose to compete in this race. He was one of the older drivers in this event. To me, he was very, very old. He was 46. I reminisce and laugh at how everyone at the track looked old next to me.

Fortunately for me he did not win the mechanic's race. I am certain that if he had won, I would have never got my car back from him. It was a hilarious moment when he pulled into the pits after the race ended. He slid deftly out of the car with a smile second to none I had ever seen on his face. Immediately after his feet hit the ground, he turned to Nick Moore, my future brother-in-law and member of my pit crew, and said loudly and proudly, "WOW! I think I found something better than sex!" Nick still laughingly recounts this incident when the subject of racing or my dad comes up.

The fall and winter of 1973 meant school and work and drinking, school and work and drinking, wash, rinse, repeat. Pioneer 66 kept all three mechanic's bays busy, and I was constantly doing brake jobs, tire repair, new tires, tune-ups, engine overhauls, carburetor rebuilds, u-joint replacements etc., etc., etc.

Car repair ignorance was never an issue with me. If I didn't know what I was doing, I plunged head-first into it, and if I broke it, I would replace the broken part and move ahead like it was broken all along. Experience can be an expensive teacher. In those days, a sizable number of car repair "victims" unwittingly paid to educate me due to my lack of knowledge and/or experience. However, for themost part, I was relatively efficient at my repair tasks.

Dad, once again, seriously surprised me in November of 1973. He was an avid reader of the now-defunct Rocky Mountain News. It was a large, tabloid-style newspaperfrom Denver. I always liked that newspaper. It seemed far more pertinent than the larger, standard layout of the Denver Post. In fact, the Denver Post eventually acquired the Rocky Mountain News and quietly buried it. Too bad. It was a worthy newspaper that succumbed to competitionand economic pressure from the Denver Post.

Even though we lived in Montrose, Dad subscribed to the Rocky Mountain News and used the classified-ad section to find the old cars and trucks he used to "invest" in. This was how people did things in those days. There was no internet or other multimedia sales outlet(s) for personal use. If you wanted to buy or sell something, you visited the newspaper and looked at the classified advertisements. I am glad he did. It seems he was keeping his eyes open for stock cars.

At that time, the Denver area had a couple of stock car tracks. There was Englewood and Colorado National Speedway (CNS) in Erie, just north of Denver. He found anadvertisement for a custom-built 1957 Ford stock car.

Colorado National Speedway had moved to late models and phased out the older cars. Most were relegated to the junk yards as they were beaten to pieces. However, this old Ford was in *excellent* shape. It did not have running gear but was fully ready to race if you dropped in an engine and transmission. Plus, it had a well-built, heavy-duty, tandem axle trailer to haul it.

Dad had me take a weekend off from the filling station, and we drove to Denver and looked at the car. It was loveat first sight for me. It needed some paint, but the professionally built roll cage, chassis/suspension, and body were in excellent condition. Dad paid $950.00 for the car and the trailer. The car had NASCAR-quality racing wheels and tires. These alone probably cost more than we paid for the car when they were new.

After one look, I wanted to hug this car. It was truly love at first sight for me. I could not have been moreexcited had it been a new Ferrari. Dad paid the owner, and we hauled it back to Montrose on its trailer. Though heavy, it towed like a dream. Dad felt the trailer alone was worth
$500.00. He, surprisingly, agreed to pick up the cost of the car with the following provisions:

- **I continue to work at the station (he felt it keptme out of trouble).**
- **I get my grade average up to 3.0. (Like this wasever going to happen?)**
- **I build an engine with my own money, capable ofpowering this professionally built car. (I loved it!)**

Though I didn't realize it then, Dad was smarter than I thought he was. His plan to help keep me away from trouble worked. I was thoroughly caught up in building the racing engine and preparing the stock car for opening day in 1974. These preparations kept me busy every waking hour of the day. Between this, school, and working evenings/weekends at Pioneer 66, it monopolized my time.I was still drinking heavily, but he or Mom never knew it. Itwas mostly on the weekends after I left work.

Dad "roped" Del Wiesner into sponsoring the new car. Del was impressed enough with my performance during my first year of racing and with the car we bought in Denver, that he took the sponsorship seriously. He pitched in a sizable amount of money and expertise in building the engine for the car.

I spent a large part of my disposable income building the engine and finishing the necessary tasks to get the car ready for the first race of the season. It was at the Delta County Raceway in Delta, Colorado. Unfortunately, the Montrose track went out of business in 1973.

The new racing engine turned out better than I could have hoped. We had it professionally balanced and used high-end racing parts to build it. Del taught me a tremendous amount about building high performanceengines.

After I overhauled an engine, my goal was to have it start immediately the first time it was prompted to do so. This meant having the valve and ignition timing set perfectly, the carburation correct, and everything in proper order and functional. This engine did not disappoint. I had an abundance of butterflies as I pressed the starter. It immediately roared to life. I had a ton of hours invested in fabricating and building my own custom exhaust headers from scratch, and they sounded fantastic!

Del's construction company used a dark green and gold paint scheme on all his equipment. He had an enormous shop with a paint booth. He unquestionably spent more money than it was worth to professionally paint the new car using his green and gold scheme.

He even went so far as to do professional, gold leaf lettering for the number 16, my name, and Del Wiesner Trucking Company. The car was gorgeous. What's more, itran as good or better than it looked! I never thought I wouldhave a car this magnificent, and I also never imagined how fast I could utterly destroy it!

~3~ EVERYONE GOES TO SEE THE CRASHES!

1974 turned out to be an incredibly eventful year. Richard Nixon resigned from the Presidency due to the Watergate scandal, and the Vietnam War finally came to an end, leaving the United States grappling with the aftermath of a conflict that could have been concluded in a few months if not for corrupt politics and flawed foreign policies.

The year also saw the OPEC oil embargo, as Middle Eastern countries halted oil production, straining the West's obsession with cars, boats, motorcycles, and airplanes. The United States' fervent love for automobiles became a significant issue amid the embargo, which created immensestress for a nation deeply enamored with its oil-consuming passions. Despite this, 1974 was my best year of racing andthe year I married my true love, whom I had known for only a few weeks. Indeed, 1974 was a wild year!

The oil embargo was particularly alarming for a car enthusiast teenager. While Montrose did not experience long gas lines, CBS News Anchor Walter Cronkite's coverage highlighted the severe shortages across the nation with scenes of frustrated motorists waiting in long lines for fuel. Despite the increased fuel costs, racing continued unabated. It's often said that "love always finds a way," a sentiment that, while typically reserved for deeply spiritual or romantic matters, also perfectly encapsulates the passion of racing.

My close friend, Nick Moore, a year younger than me, shared my love for racing. He grew up in Cedaredge, Colorado, a small mountain town near Delta, Colorado, where the Delta racetrack was located. He rarely missed a race during his teenage years. In 1973, Nick's father, Lee, bought the Ideal Thriftway food market, which led them to move to Montrose.

Nick and I bonded over my race car, and he eagerly volunteered to join the pit crew, partly for the ride to Delta on race nights. In this style of dirt-track racing, pit crews didn't perform complex, choreographed stops for fuel and tires. Instead, they focused on pulling out *'banged-in- fenders,'* tire changes, securing food and drinks, or relayinginformation about other racers.

Opening night on May 4th, 1974, at Delta County Raceway was a whirlwind of activity. It was a warm, picturesque Saturday evening, as spring transitioned into summer. The anticipation in the air was palpable among thespectators eager for the start of the 1974 racing season.
About 30 cars, in varying states of readiness, lined up at thetrack. The combination of exhaust fumes, burning eyes, dust, and the deafening noise of high-performance engines created a visceral rush, flooding participants with adrenaline.

Although the pit area was rife with drugs and alcohol, the atmosphere was intensely euphoric. I saw no reason to

dilute this chaotic reality with alcohol and risk overshadowing the intense thrill of the moment.

The exhilaration of high RPM racing engines is unmatched. The mechanical symphony of a racing engine—from its guttural rumbling to its high-speed wail— surpasses any philharmonic crescendo. Drawing out every ounce of hidden horsepower floods a racer with a sense of superiority, knowing your are flirting with the unyielding laws of physics.

The collective roar of multiple engines at peak RPM creates an adrenaline rush that surpasses any artificial high. When racing is in your blood, its allure is irresistible. It's an addiction like no other.

On May 4th, 1974, I was ecstatic and eager to hot lap the new, untested #16. The smell of fresh paint on the car was still detectable as we unloaded and made final checks

The Author and # 16 on May 4th, 1974

and adjustments. The sun was still smiling broadly on the raceway, not requiring the track lights for at least another hour or two. I wore a white pocket tee shirt with the number 16 prominently displayed on my back and white corduroy slacks. I decided this would be my trademark; while Johnny Cash was the "man in black," I was the "kid in white." It's ironic that I chose white, given how perpetually greasy and filthy I was from working at Pioneer66 or on various vehicles. Despite the track dust and grime that instantly sullied my white attire, I insisted on wearing it.

The initial hot lap session was the first time I had driven the car outside of the alley behind our house or Del Wiesner's driveway. Driving it at home was difficult due to the deafening noise of the open exhaust headers and the car's lack of street legality. However, tonight was our time!

I quickly pushed the car to its limits during the hot lap session. I was in awe of its raw performance and agile handling. It deftly maneuvered the 3/8 mile, high banked, dirt oval remarkably well. The engine roared, smooth and balanced, showcasing the hours I spent building the engine and crafting the custom exhaust headers. I was incredibly proud of the engine's performance.

By the 5th lap, I had adapted to its handling, enjoying its perfect oversteer and responsive throttle. Oversteer, where the rear of the car slides outward during a turn, is controlled with the accelerator pedal. Oval track racing relies almost entirely on the accelerator pedal and not the steering wheel. Understeer, where the front wheels slide and the car continues straight, is dangerous and quickly leads to a crash. Thankfully, this car had a very manageable oversteer, making it feel as if the chassis-setup in Denver was expertly done. The car and I became one with the track, with it responding instinctively to my will.

After about 10 laps, I pitted before the time trials. Dad ran to the car excitedly waving the stopwatch in his hand and exclaimed, "Each lap was faster than the previous one!" He then gave me a look of approval that I seldom ever saw from him. As I came to a stop in the pits, he nodded slowly and said, "I am impressed, son."

My time trial went exceptionally well, placing me almost at the back of the FAST heat race. I was not just among the "big boys" as Dad called them; I was one of the fastest. The first race was the FAST heat, consisting of 10 laps. Despite my utter disbelief, the car performed masterfully, and I finished second. After the heat race, several drivers approached, admiring the car and asking questions. I was bursting with pride. Dad and Nick were equally thrilled.

The slow heat race followed, consisting of the slower cars from the time trials. I was too absorbed in sharing my excitement with Dad, Nick, and the pit crew to pay any attention to this race. My confidence soared, a combination of youthful exuberance and high testosterone levels, which proved to be a potentially deadly mix.

Next was the fast trophy dash, also 10 laps but for a large trophy. The car and I proved to be perfectly in sync. I was an exhilarated passenger as the car gracefully and effortlessly seemed to slip quickly by the other cars. On the final lap, I pushed even harder and overtook one of the fastest cars to win the trophy dash. During my victory lap with the checkered flag, I was awash in endorphins and an unparalleled euphoria.

After the trophy dash, even more drivers came to congratulate me, further fueling my sense of pride and invincibility. I found the holy grail of racing and was on a high beyond anything alcohol had ever provided. I eagerly anticipated the next race, the 25-lap main event, where first place could earn up to $150, a magnificent sum of money for a 17-year-old racer in 1974.

During the main event, the car was again in its element, and I maneuvered toward the front of the pack. On about the 10th lap, Ralph Pagone in his screaming orange 1957 Chevy blocked my progress as he and another car fought for second place. My frustration grew as I remained stuck in 4th place, unable to pass due to their side-by-side battle. Unfortunately, my desire to prove our superiority, coupled with the car's willingness, pushed me to the limit of my patience.

The Delta track was perfectly situated adjacent to a large adobe hill, where spectators set up blankets and lawn chairs to watch the races from above. On the track's front stretch, a six-foot high dirt bank separated the bottom of the hill from the track. Most tracks use steel fences, stacked tires, or other strong barriers between the race cars and spectators. Delta didn't need such barriers. They had the adobe berm. Due to the relatively steep angle of the hill above the berm, spectators were restricted from sitting below a certain point, ensuring a safe distance between the cars and people. This created an absolutely perfect spectator setup for any racetrack, anywhere—offering unparalleled views and safety.

On about the 20th lap, I grew frustrated with Ralph Pagone and his ongoing battle with another, clearly inferior racer. Car #16 decided it was time for some undeniable magic. You must understand, the car was eager and encouraged me to act. I observed Ralph and his opponent for several laps. They would come out of corner # 4 high and then drop low on the home stretch, heading into corner #1. What else would they do? This is the natural movementon any oval track… God's physics. Even though both cars were low, *there were still two cars side by side on a relatively narrow track.*

I quickly calculated that the track was wide enough on the home stretch to fit three cars. I would come out of #4 ontheir rear bumpers, and when they dropped back down, the car and I agreed to effortlessly slip by, astonishing them with our superior speed and agility. I should have never listened to that damn car.

On the 23rd lap, I executed my dreadfully absurd plan. As I accelerated hard to pass both cars, we drifted far higher than I expected due to my sheer ignorance and inexperience. About half way down the front stretch of the track, the right front corner of the car planted itself violently into the adobe safety berm, creating a massive gash in the steep adobe wall. ***Physics always prevails.***

We were moving so fast that the car instantly exited thedivot, soaring high through the air and then flipping violently end over end approximately 2.5 times right in front of God, the spectators, and my parents.

We came to rest upside down, alarmingly close to the lowest tier of spectators. I don't recall hearing or feeling anything during the crash—nothing. I just woke up upside down, strapped tightly by the racing harness/seat belts. The crash was so brutal that the racing seat broke completely loose from its mount and separated from the roll cage. The seat and I were dangling upside-down, held only by the racing harness attached solidly to the roll cage supports.

I was trying to gather my senses when someone reached in and released the racing harness. The seat and I fell about 6 inches onto the inner roof of the car, head-first. They then pushed the seat off me and pulled me out of the car by my shoulders. There were no modern practices of using backboards and safety equipment—they just dragged me out. Fortunately, my neck wasn't broken, though there certainly wasn't much in my head that could have been damaged. I proved I was a brainless 17-year-old teenager.

Despite extreme disorientation, I quickly stood up next to the car. People were gathering around me. I vaguely remember the public address system announcing that I appeared to be okay and then hearing the crowd cheer wildly. I turned to face the car, which was upside down and crumpled into a partial ball. It looked utterly destroyed. I felt as though I had violently murdered my new best friend.

To this day, I don't know what happened next except that I blacked out and collapsed. I woke up a few moments later as they were loading me into the ambulance. *I felt like a total loser once I was in the ambulance.*

The ride to Delta Hospital was quick. They advised me to stay quiet even though I wanted to talk. I had a splitting headache, and my shins hurt. During the violent end-over- end flipping, my shins had smashed into the underside of the sheet metal dashboard, causing gashes that bled and mixed with dust and dirt from the track, forming a muddy barrier impeding blood flow.

I spent about an hour and 30 minutes in the emergency room for a check-up. The ER doctor performed basic tests and asked me several questions. Apparently, I passed. The nurse cleaned and bandaged my shins, and the doctor told me to go home and rest. The fact that this could have endedfar worse didn't escape me. But I was 17 years old and felt invincible. Ironically, I had no idea that I was about to experience the biggest life change, ever.

The nurse wheeled me to the exit door of the hospital. Outside, I saw Nick Moore, my mom, and a few others. Dad was taking the wrecked car back to Montrose. Standing beside Nick was a diminutive, strikingly attractive girl with a dark complexion. Her prominent, beautiful cheekbones and soul-piercing chocolate-brown eyes radiated with beauty. Flowing dark brown hair cascaded over her shoulders resting gracefully on her back. She was the perfect package of beauty, grace, and class.

As I stood up and stepped away from the wheelchair, she and I locked eyes, and I was instantly struck with a torrent of emotions beyond any I had ever felt. My heart fluttered as I was entirely certain I was looking into the eyes of an angel.

I knew that very moment she would be the love of my life. I married that girl a few months later. You can't make this up because the dates don't lie. Our first time seeing each other after the races that night was Friday, May 4, 1974. We were married on August 17th, 1974.

~4~

THE LOVE OF MY LIFE

Her name was Evangeline Elsie Marie Aguilar, but she preferred to be called Vangie. Deep down, I always knew I would marry a girl with a unique and beautiful name. In fact, once I started noticing girls, I often considered their names, and if a girl had a common name, I lost interest immediately. No matter how foolish it may sound, that was the truth.

Vangie had been Nick's next-door neighbor for less than a year. I think Nick really liked her, but whether he knew it or not, the feeling was far from mutual. They worked together at the Ideal Thriftway food store, but she showed no interest in Nick. Anyone who knows Vangie will tell you that she is very decisive.

Vangie's dad was a gold miner who worked in the stunning and majestic San Juan Mountains for the now- defunct Idarado Mining Company. This captivating young lady was born in Ouray, Colorado, in a granite block building from the late 1880s. It is now the Ouray County Historical Museum and is a must-see if you are ever fortunate enough to visit Ouray.

I still tease her about being born in a museum. Ouray (pronounced You-Ray) is a small, historic mining town nestled in the breathtaking San Juan Mountains of Southwest Colorado. It is called "The Switzerland of America" due to its magnificent, snow-capped, jagged peaks. When Vangie was three years old, the Aguilar family moved to Ridgway, Colorado, about 10 miles north of Ouray.

When Vangie was 15, her father, Alex, faced a life- altering event. While riding his motorcycle in Ridgway, he was struck by a Land Rover driven by an aging man with poor vision. The collision nearly killed Alex and left him with severe injuries. He spent many weeks in and out of hospitals in Grand Junction and Montrose. Surgeons performed a relatively new procedure at the time, piecing together his right leg and ankle with plates and screws. Despite the intense pain and a noticeable limp that would last for the rest of his life, Alex, a tough and resilient man, fought through the adversity and continued to walk.

In 1973, the Aguilar family had moved from Ridgway to East Main Street in Montrose to be closer to doctors and hospitals. They bought the house next door to the Moore's. This led Vangie to get a job at the food market owned by Lee Moore, Nick's dad.

Vangie had two younger twin sisters named Bernadine and Bernadette and three older sisters: Linda, Alice, and the eldest, Gloria. All of them were very pretty girls. However, Vangie was the gem of all the sisters. She was modest, virtuous, and incredibly smart. This is not to say the other sisters lacked these qualities; they all possessed them to varying degrees. However, in my opinion, Vangie was the complete package.

Oddly, the age spread of her five sisters was almost identical to my own five siblings. Nick (Moore) was also sweet on Bernadette, who was three years younger than him. They eventually married and are still together to this day.

The Sunday morning after my big crash, I was supposed to work at the filling station/garage. I had to call my boss, Walt Hull, to inform him I would be a few hours late. He was not particularly happy about this but had no choice because every bone in my body ached. I was bruised across my chest from the racing harness restraining my flailing body and the weight of the broken racing seat. My shins were gashed, bruised, and hurting, and I still had a terrible headache. In 1974, this would probably be considered a severe concussion. But since I wasn't vomiting, it couldn't be serious, right?

No matter how rough I felt, the poor stock car was in far worse shape. Quite surprisingly, Dad didn't go golfing that Sunday. He was already working on the car. Wait a minute…Did I just say that Dad didn't go golfing on a Sunday morning? This was unheard of and shocking. No golf game today? Unreal! He was in the backyard furiously dismantling the stock car. It was Sunday morning, and I had no interest in helping as I nursed my wounds. My body ached from the wreck, and I could not get that exotic, dark- complected girl out of my mind.

My current employer was Walter Henry Hull, who owned Hull Petroleum, Pioneer 66 and Cedar Creek 66 on the other side of town. Duane Morris had been leasing the station from the Hulls, but he retired due to health issues, so Walt assumed control of the facility.

Walt was smart, excitable, and currently focused on promoting tire sales. Olin Davidson, the manager of the service station, nicknamed him "Shakey" because he always appeared to be sporting about 23 cups of espresso in him. Walt had a "thing" for tire sales. They were apparently very lucrative for Hull Petroleum.

He had recently renamed the three-bay garage and filling station where I worked to Pioneer 66. He advertised heavily and pushed a "grand re-opening," celebrating the new name change and a new emphasis on tire sales. People were encouraged via local radio advertising to come by for free (stale) donuts and fill out an entry for a free tank of gasthat was awarded daily.

I managed to show up to work at about noon that Sunday. Believe me when I say it wasn't my first choice. It was incredibly fortuitous that I did so because later that afternoon, a cute gold Datsun 1200 with white racing stripes and mag wheels drove into the gas station for gas. It was Vangie's car. By working at Ideal Thriftway food store as a checker, she purchased the near-new Datsun and then added the little mag wheels and racing stripes. As cute as the little Datsun was, she was far cuter.

My heart skipped about four beats when she pulled into the gas bay. She had never purchased gas here that I knew of. We were a "full-service" station and charged more than the self-serve stations. Everyone our age would go to the self-serve stations to save 6 or 7 cents a gallon by pumping their own gas.

I put $1.00 worth of gas in the little Datsun. She wasn't necessarily being cheap. Gas was 38 cents a gallon. This probably gave the tiny little Datsun nearly half a tank of fuel. I tried to make small talk, but she was cool and reserved, making it clear she was there solely for the gas. She took a moment to complete an entry form for the daily gas giveaway promotion and then immediately departed, leaving me sullen and heartbroken.

She does not believe me to this day, but that evening, Olin Davidson and I drew for the free tank of gas for Monday. Olin mixed up the twenty or thirty entry forms and put them in a 2-gallon bucket. We had done this several times previously because the grand reopening was a 10-day event. I reached high into the bucket and dug around the entry forms. The first one I pulled out was none other than Evangeline Elsie Marie Aguilar.

To be fair, had I not pulled her name out on the first try, I am sure I would have cheated and dug it out anyway. However, as God is my witness, her name was blindly pulled out on the first try. *It was simply meant to be...*

Now I needed to muster the courage to call and inform her of her incredibly good fortune. Of course, there were no cell phones in 1974. I didn't wait for her to get home from work as I probably should have. I looked in the Montrose phone book and found the number for Ideal Thriftway food market and immediately called with the news of her astonishing stroke of luck. The conversation was brief. Lee Moore answered the phone.

"Could I speak to Vangie Aguilar, please?" "Who's calling?"

"Mark Gregg at Pioneer – 66." He put the phone down. I could hear muffled talking and background noises as someone called out for Vangie. It took a several minutes for her to get to the phone. I am sure she was busy at the cash register, and someone had to fill in for her.

"This is Vangie." She sounded concerned but still had the voice of an angel.

My voice was supposed to be manly, firm, and confident. I'm not sure it was any of these. I was as nervous as a hog in a pork processing facility. My pre-made plan was simple and effective.

"This is Mark Gregg. I am calling to tell you that you won either a fill-up of gas or a free trip to the Drive-In movie with me next Friday evening in our daily drawing at Pioneer 66." There was a deafening pause.

"I would like the tank of gas." was the curt but playful reply. I was stunned.

Thinking quickly, I responded, "Sorry, but you have to take both." Another pause.

"Can I answer when I come to get the gas?" "Perfect," I answered.

"When can I expect you here?"

"Thursday, after school?" she answered again in her cool, reserved voice.

I replied with unrestrained fervor. "Great, I will see you then!" Success! How could she turn me down now, *right*?

Dad continued to work on the race car every day after work. I avoided it like the plague. I could not get Vangie off my mind and certainly had no interest in helping with the post-mortem on my car.

The first few days after the crash, I took notice of how diligently Dad worked on the car. He painstakingly stripped it down, removing the smashed, unusable parts and straightening, bending, and reworking the extensively damaged items that still had life.

Thursday finally rolled around. I eagerly rushed to work immediately after school. I could not take a chance of missing Vangie. I watched the gas bays intently because I had to be the one who attended to her when she came in. Sure enough. She arrived for the gas as she said she would. My heart began pounding as it had on our previous rendezvous.

She pulled into the gas lane and remained inside the little Datsun. This was normal because we were a full-service station, and we did the filling. She rolled down the driver's window as I ran to her car.

"I would like my fill-up from the contest." She was staggeringly beautiful to me. Her dark, exotic, deeply piercing eyes looked right into me. My heart was racing because I knew my life would never be complete if she turned me down for the drive-in. Every fiber of my being told me I was supposed to be with this girl. I quickly put the gas nozzle into Datsun's gas tank and returned to the driver's window.

"Soooo… You know that if you take this gas, you are required to go to the drive-in with me, right?"

Her eyes turned mischievous. With a coy smile, she said, "Does your boss know about this?"

"Of course. It is all part of the contest." I replied jokingly.

"Sounds a little creepy to me." She just sat there waiting for me to say something. I was squirming. Luckily, the gas nozzle clicked off, so I ran back, removed it, put it back on the pump, and then returned to her driver's window.

"So, are you coming with me to the drive-in tomorrow night?" My voice cracked a bit. I was dying inside.

She looked at me for a moment. She had smiling eyes. "Aren't you supposed to clean my windshield?"

"Depends on whether you will go to the drive-in with me or not," I replied, grinning as I started wiping down the Datsun's windshield with the sponge and squeegee. When I finished cleaning the windshield, she started Datsun's engine. My heart leaped into my throat. ***IS SHE TURNING ME DOWN?*** I was panicking.

"Yes, I will go to the drive-in with you tomorrow evening." She put the Datsun into gear and started to ease forward. I did a fist pump in my mind. YES!!! She said YES. She was going on a date with me!!!

"I will pick you up at about 7:00 at your house. Is that okay?"

"Sure, that works." She gave me a smile that made my heart flutter even more wildly as she eased out of the pump bay.

I walked on air the entire day Friday, at school. After school ended, I drove my 1966 GTO down to the auto parts store to pick up some parts Dad asked me to bring home for the race car.

Once home, I asked Dad if I could use ***his*** car for the drive-in movie that night. He looked unquestionably annoyed at me.

"Why aren't you going to the races in Delta tonight?' His voice was openly laced with irritation. He could not understand why I wasn't going to the races. It was Friday night, and we always went to the races in Delta, whether I was racing or not.

"Believe it or not, I have a date tonight." This was an odd statement for him to digest. I had never dated before this.

"What's her name?" He asked cynically, almostimplying that I was lying to him.

"Vangie." I didn't offer any additional information. He would flip if he knew she was Hispanic. Dad could be extremely prejudiced and voiced it regularly. In fact, as bad as it was that I was ditching the race car for a date, it would be even worse if he found out she wasn't his idea of the perfect girl.

"Why do you need my car… What's wrong with your GTO?"

"The seats are white vinyl and absolutely filthy because I have been getting parts in it. I don't have time to clean it now." I paused and looked him in his eyes. "I don'twant to pick Vangie up and get her clothes dirty on our firstdate." This was the truth. The seats of the GTO fully testified to my lack of personal hygiene and love affair withgrease and oil.

"Fine. Use my car. But I hope you get your interest back in the race car. Del Wiesner spent a lot of money to sponsor you, and one race is not what he or anyone else expected from you and this car."

I snapped back at him. "Is the car even salvageable?" In retrospect, I should have thanked him for loaning me his car and not said anything further. My response caused him to erupt as only he could.

"HELL, YES, THE CAR IS FIXABLE!" As was often the case, he was yelling right in my face. "If you paid any attention, you would have seen that I have been working on it all week. In fact, I could use a hand from YOU to fix YOUR damn car." His eyes were crazy angry. This always scared me. Deep down, I think I knew this was coming. I had been avoiding him AND the backyard like the plague.

"Dad, I will work on the stock car this weekend. I'm sorry I haven't been helping." I tried to sound as repentant as possible. In reality, I hadn't felt like even looking at the car. Dad grunted something under his breath and stormed out of the room.

At least he agreed to let me use his car. It was a plush 1969 Ford station wagon. It had bench seats and was clean and comfortable. I thought it was probably the perfect date car. Vangie would obviously prefer the plush, clean seats of the station wagon over the greasy seats of the GTO.

I arrived at Vangie's house at 7:00, as promised. I cleaned up as best I could for the date. Considering I was a skinny, often disheveled mess, I felt good about how I looked that night. I even combed my hair and wore white socks!

I knocked nervously on the front door. Her Dad, Alex, answered the door. As with Vangie and her sisters, he was not tall. He was considered a small man and years of hard work in the mines, plus having a barbell set he worked with daily, provided him with ample biceps and a barrel chest. Frankly, he was a walking muscle. The bicep in either arm was more powerful than my legs and Vangie's little Datsun combined. He could be very intimidating. He opened the door and just stared at me.

"Is Vangie here?" I asked timidly.

He gave me an intense once-over and said, "Who wants to know?"

I generated all the courage I could muster and EXTENDED my right hand. "I am Mark Gregg. Vangie and I are seeing a movie tonight." He slowly shook my hand.

Dad always taught me to shake a hand with purpose andwith as firm a grip as possible. Alex was obviously taught this, also. I was certain the small bones in my hand were fractured beyond repair from the death grip he put on it.

He turned and hollered to Vangie that I was there. He then asked me to step inside while waiting for her. I felt a wave of relief flow over me when his facial muscles relaxed, and his look of abject hatred melted to intense dislike. Her mother, Cordie, was a very pretty woman. She was extremely gracious to me, and I immediately liked her.

Vangie came out of her room a few minutes later. She was dressed casually and had her big mountain boots on. I think she wore them everywhere, always. I marveled at how pretty she was. She said goodbye to her mom and Dad as we stepped out of the house. She was noticeably taken aback as we stepped into their driveway.

"Where is your GTO?" she asked with obvious concern bordering on irritation.

"It broke down today, so I borrowed my dad's car." I could tell the station wagon did not sit well with her. I was now seriously questioning my judgement in bringing it. Not knowing her, I did not realize how classy and dignified she was.

We went to the Star Drive-In theatre, which is still in business to this day. It probably holds a record for one of the longest-running drive-in movie theatres in the country. I don't remember the movie we saw. I don't remember any specific conversation. I just remember sitting next to Vangie and feeling like the universe and I were in sync.

The movie ended, and as the credits rolled, the cars around us began to lumber out. I steered the station wagon onto the main road. I glanced over at Vangie sitting next to me, and in that instant, our eyes locked and we shared a brief and amazing kiss— our first. It was spontaneous, catching me completely off guard, but it was a moment I would never forget.

However, the excitement was short-lived. Instead of going straight to her house, I decided to take a little detour, enjoying a drive with her. Vangie had other plans. "I have to work all day tomorrow at the store," she said, slowly sliding back to her side of the car. "Could you take me home?"

I was floored. One second, we were sharing a magical first kiss, and the next, she was asking to go home, leaving me in flames, fire, and smoke from the rejection. It wasn't that she seemed upset—she wasn't. I just couldn't understand how the moment had shifted so fast.

"Maybe we can take a drive in your GTO when you get it fixed." I could tell by the mildly sarcastic tone of her voice that she did not believe for a moment that it was broken. The good news is she left the door open for anotherdate. Woo Hoo! Life was, indeed, still livable.

We got back to her house a little after 11:00 PM. The lights were on in the front room. As I walked her to the front door, her mom saw us coming and opened the door, inviting me in. We sat down in the comfortable, nicely decorated front room. Their house was quite new. I was used to our much older home. I liked the style and brightness of the newer homes.

Cordie asked about the movie, racing, and several othertopics. About 5 minutes into our conversation, Vangie promptly stood up, said she was tired, and walked to her bedroom, throwing a curt goodnight over her shoulder before her door closed. It was surreal.

In retrospect, I obviously should have taken the hint and left. However, her mom and I talked for at least 20 more minutes. We would have talked even longer, but I became uncomfortable at Vangie bolting off to bed with me sitting there. I told Cordie that I also had to work the next day and needed rest. I did like her mom. She was a nice lady.

The following day, work lumbered on like a bad toothache. All I could think about was Vangie. I called her immediately after getting home from work. We talked onthe phone for over an hour. That was 50 years ago, and we have spoken every day since then. I told her the GTO was filthy and I needed to clean it up before she could ride in it. She volunteered to come over to the house and help clean it.

I thought it was an excellent idea and invited her to the house.

Sunday afternoon, she came to the house and helped clean the GTO. Okay, okay… SHE CLEANED THE GTO. She worked her tail off using Comet cleanser, water, spray cleaner, sponges, rags, and several other cleaning items. She scrubbed and scrubbed the dark gray vinyl seats until they were white again! The interior looked almost newwhen she finished. I couldn't believe it.

In retrospect, I honestly remember exactly what I was thinking about the rest of that week:

Monday – Vangie Tuesday – Vangie Wednesday – Vangie

Thursday – Vangie Friday – Vangie Saturday – Vangie

Are you seeing a pattern here?

If I wasn't with her, we were on the phone together. The race car? Well, Dad worked on it far more than I did. In fact, HE prepared it for the races that next Friday night with very little help from me. He did an amazing job of putting it back together. It didn't even look bad. It wasn't the spotless, dent-free show car it was before the first night, but it came back together nicely. The problem now was a simple one… It was now time for me to perform again.

Was I ready?

~5~ MARRIAGE AT SIXTEEN?

We trailered the race car to the Delta track that Friday night and unloaded it. Vangie and Nick drove to the races in Vangie's splendid little Datsun. Before the time trials, I did a few hot laps in the repaired stock car. Was I nervous? Not at all. Well, maybe just a little. I was also thrilled. I loved the exhilaration of racing.

I pulled out of the pits and wasted no time testing the repair. I spun out between turns 1 and 2 on the first hard lap. On a banked oval track, there are two straight stretches, the front and the back, and two U-shaped corners at each end. Duh! It's an oval. However, the U-shaped corners are called turns 1 and 2 on one end of the track and turns 3 and
4 on the other end. The spin-out happened so fast it shocked me. Fortunately, I missed the light poles and everything else and could continue the hot laps.

I pulled back onto the track, regained my composure, and hit it hard again. I spun out, this time between turns 3 and 4. I pulled into the pits, where Dad was waiting apprehensively.

He didn't wait for me to get out of the car. "What's the problem?" he yelled into the car.

"This thing handles like crap!" I hollered over the track noise.

"What's it doing?"

"For one, it's loose and goosey. Secondly, it's fighting me all the way. It fights me under power, it fights me in the corners, it doesn't feel right at all."

I slid out of the driver's window, and we canvassed the car, looking for anything obvious that could be causing these issues. He assured me the frame wasn't bent because he measured it in every possible way it could be measured. The roll cage in a stock car is designed to keep the chassis rigid. It's connected to the frame in several spots and made of heavy steel pipe with angles and radiuses to make it extremely strong.

In stock cars, the roll cages are not just about driver safety. They're designed to make the frame rigid so that the interaction of the track is with the suspension and not unwanted frame twisting or instability. When I went end over end, the roll cage and the frame absorbed the shock and stayed rigid. The rest of the body and chassis took an absolute beating.

Dad checked tire pressures and did more measurements, ultimately declaring the car fine. This didn't sit well with me because if the car was fine, it made me the common denominator for poor performance. I knew how he thought. He wasn't happy with me seeing Vangie and seemingly losing interest in racing.

The time trials were awful. I didn't even qualify for the top half of the field. I was in the slow heat race and the semi-main event. Even then, I did poorly. The car fought every move I made. I'm certain it acted out of spite to pay me back for the damage I inflicted on it during the wreck. Where was the amazing, mind-blowing, self-driving fighterjet that won the race a few weeks prior?

The high point of the night? The trophy presentation for that night's trophy dash. Before the presentation, Jack Hawkins, the President of the DCRA (Delta Country Racing Association), asked me to accompany him to the front stretch of the track as the trophies were presented. He didn't give me a hint as to why I was supposed to be there.

I followed him and was completely shocked when they presented me with one of the largest trophies I've ever won. It was engraved, "DCRA MOST SPECTACULAR CRASH." It was an over 3-foot tall trophy featuring an upside-down car, and it drew wild applause from the stands as I accepted it and kissed the trophy queen.

Other than receiving the trophy, the night was a huge bust. Dad was dark and surly on the ride home as we towed the stock car trailer behind his pickup. He made a special effort to assure me that the car was fine. He wouldn't say it then, but I knew exactly what he was thinking. It was my fault I did so poorly; the car had nothing to do with it.

The daily phone calls to and from Vangie increased, and we were now seeing each other every single day, even if only for a few minutes. We enjoyed each other's company and seemed fully in sync. As much as I wanted to be with Vangie continuously, I had to dedicate some time to the race car this week. I wouldn't let Dad accuse me of poor performance when I knew beyond a shadow of adoubt that the car was the culprit.

We made several small changes to the chassis and fixed many minor items Dad had missed before the last race. Dad enjoyed working on the car but made it sound like a major imposition. I didn't care. So long as he didn't blame me for the bad showing, I could put up with his crappy attitude. Unfortunately, everything changed the next Friday night.

We were too late to do hot laps because Dad got home from work late. I had to do time trials without a practice lap. The car and I performed abysmally, maybe worse than the prior week. I ran the heat race and trophy dash, coming in last on one and then spinning out and leaving the race onthe other. The semi-main event (I was with the slow cars again) was just as bad. Tension was rapidly building Dad and I.

Observing his tension-filled countenance irritated me. His jaw was jutting, and his eyes looked meaner than a junkyard dog. When I pulled into the pits after each race, he slowly shook his head. I'm certain he didn't know he was doing it. His disdain and suppressed anger involuntarily boiled over into his physical actions.

On the way home, he wasted no time finally saying what had been blatantly on his mind both weeks. He enflamed my temper by making me sound like a poor,helpless invalid.

"Son, that wreck would have unnerved the best racer out there." He paused to ensure he had the proper amount of forced condolence in his voice. "I think you've lost your nerve. I don't believe the car is the problem."

I snapped and instantly retorted with fierce conviction, "THAT IS TOTAL BULLSHIT!" My anger reached a crescendo. "THE CAR HANDLED PERFECTLY THE FIRST RACE AND NOW HANDLES LIKE A TOTAL PIECE OF SHIT."

Dad was thoroughly shocked at my response, and he should have been. You see, I NEVER talked back to him like this. I knew better. His temper was bad, and when confronted, it was much worse.

He looked over from the driver's seat of the pickup and stared at me for a quick moment with a completely stunned look on his face. Complete, awkward, silence ensued for several miles. He was not sure what to say, and frankly, I had nothing more to say to him on this subject. I knew the problem was due to the wreck screwing up the car's chassis,not because I had lost my nerve.

That night after we arrived home, I called Vangie, and we talked for a couple of hours. She knew how frustrated I was. We were becoming closer by the day and discussing more and more personal issues with each other. A bond was growing between us that was becoming stronger by theday.

My explosive reaction to Dad while towing back to Montrose the previous night affected him harder than I realized. I never yelled at him before and especially never used profanities. Doing both and then shutting my mouth served me well in this situation. It could have gone wrong. Way wrong. But it didn't. That week, Dad took it upon himself to take the car to Warner Alignment in Montrosefor a second opinion.

Joe Warner was the curmudgeonly, sloppy, bald, world-weary proprietor of a front-end alignment company that had been around Montrose for as long as I could remember. His dilapidated shop and alignment equipment seemed prehistoric compared to the other alignment shops, and the inside of the garage was filthy and strewn with the remnants of car repairs from what looked like decades earlier. The building had a distinctive, permanent smell of axle grease and thick, cheap cigar smoke that wasborderline repulsive.

Dad took the car to him not because of the wisdom from age or Joe's extensive experience but because he had the reputation of being the cheapest chassis guy in town. It turned out to be the best move he could have ever made.Joe was good. No, Joe was amazing! His 40+ years of experience taught him more than most of the other alignment people in town could ever hope to know.

He spent an evening working with Dad to explain the nuances of suspension and suspension issues. He put these principles to work on the car and made extensive changesto the front end and suspension. When he finished, it was obvious that Dad and I did not know a fraction of what we thought we knew or should have known concerning suspension set-up, chassis tuning, or other items.

Late that night, Dad told me excitedly that he took the race car to Joe Warner and that Joe found a lot of things wrong. I was completely stunned when he asked me if I was willing to try the car again next Friday night.

Wow! Apparently, I needed to yell at him more often. He asked me if I would try driving it again rather than demanding that I do it and telling me that I darn sure better do it well. I graciously agreed to drive it again Friday night.

The following Friday afternoon, we exerted ourselvesto get to the track early enough to do hot laps before the time trials. Dad and I were on pins and needles concerning the car's performance. We carefully unloaded the car from the trailer, warmed the engine before I entered the track, and made a slower, precautionary run. It felt good. I then opened it up all the way. I could tell immediately, ***IT WAS BACK!!!***

Number – 16 was the car I kicked butt with on the opening night. I could instinctively visualize what I wanted, and when I opened the throttle, it did exactly what I felt in my gut. The car, once again, was an extension of my being. This is an essential factor in oval track racing. You must beconfident that the car will do what you expect under every circumstance, no matter how challenging. This car was at that point again.

Deep down in my gut, I was concerned that I would injure or kill her a second time. As with the opening night, I once again completed time trials and was paired with the FAST cars. After the big wreck, I learned a serious lesson and was far more respectful of the banks and the berm. However, I opened it up and let her have her way with the track and the other racers. We finished second in the heat race, first in the trophy dash, and third in the main event. I had an absolute blast racing the car that night.

The only thing I enjoyed more (far more) than the actual race was hitting the pits after the race and telling Dad, ***"I told you so!"*** He winced each time but gave me a smile I had seldom gotten from him growing up… One of acceptance. I actually felt some appreciation from him for the first time in my life. *It was awesome!*

Every week following that night, the car and I grew better and better together. Vangie and I experienced the same phenomena. Each week, we drew closer and missed each other's company every moment we were apart. The late spring and summer of 1974 had five modes of life for me in this order: Vangie, racing, work, eating, and Vangie.

Vangie and I finished our junior year at Montrose High School at the end of May 1974. She was a much better student than I and routinely brought A's and B's home. I finished the year with my normal "D" average, absolutely elated that I could maintain this life-long, winning scholastic trend in my junior year. School was out, and I could now visit Vangie, drink, work, and race. I mean, honestly, what more does life need?

The following weeks found me eating as many or more meals with the Aguilars as I was at my own house. Vangie's mother would make beans, chili, and homemade tortillas almost daily. I was, and still am, a Mexican food junky. I could eat it every day for every meal and never get tired of it. I never experienced true Mexican chili or homemade tortillas until meeting Vangie. You must trust me when I tell you they are amazing.

Mexican green chili is a greenish sauce or gravy made with hot, chopped Anaheim chili peppers, pork, garlic, and other ingredients. You would ladle it over eggs, meat, potatoes, vegetables, and anything else food or non-food- related. Red Chili is similar but uses beef hamburger meat and red chili powder. Both are in their own food group (you know the group I am speaking of... *AWESOME*) and can be eaten at any hour of the day or night.

Cordie and Alex treated me like royalty at their house, and I was there continuously when I wasn't working. I felt more comfortable there than I did in my own house. I was comfortable enough with them that I would finish work and go straight to their house even though I was filthy, greasy, and dirty.

In hindsight, I probably could have cleaned up a bit more before visiting them. They were very clean, organizedpeople. I am still surprised they did not complain about my lack of hygiene when I arrived after work. My connection to Cordie, Alex, and Vangie grew substantially in an incredibly short period of time.

On a late June evening in 1974, Vangie and I talked on the phone for over two hours. We were becoming so connected that talking with her was almost euphoric. That night, though, something special happened. I just knew I had to marry her. We had known each other for seven whole weeks, and if this isn't enough, nothing ever would be… **Right?**

I told her I had something special to ask her the next time we were together. She quizzed me about my intention, but I playfully eluded her questions and assured her I wouldlet her know the next time we saw each other. This was an easy thing to say because we saw each other continuously.

The following morning, she came over to our house before work. I came out to the large front porch of our big, old, gray house on 4th Street and gave her a passionate embrace and a passionate kiss. We sat on the front steps, and I got right down to business.

"I think we should get married." There was no romantic build-up, no kneeling, no fanfare. I just blurted it out. She stared at me, slightly taken aback, for a few moments before answering.

Looking at me with curious eyes she simply said, "Okay." Again, no fanfare or emotional outbursts or a romantic display of her throwing her arms around me, exclaiming her eternal, undying love and devotion for me. I didn't have a ring to give her. In fact, at the time, I did not know this was even a "thing." This was probably one of the most innocent and naïve proposals ever. The moment wasn't over yet. Besides the decision to marry, we had to solve some of life's biggest dilemmas.

"Where will we live?" She asked pointedly. I had to think for a moment. After all, a question of this magnitude requires a few moments of thought.

"Well, we both make enough money to easily afford an apartment. We can buy some used furniture and such." I was thinking, planning, and deeply strategizing as I spoke.

The "plan" seemed good to me. Vangie, on the other hand, is a true master planner and thinker. She will mull things over thoroughly before making sound judgements on most issues. In retrospect, we were truly opposites in many areas of our lives. Opposites tend to attract, and we were quite attracted to each other. This was certain.

"Let's think about this and devise a smart plan." Her sensible and reasonable response was not surprising. We agreed this would be best. We talked about things for a few more minutes, and then we both had to go to work. Those few moments on the front porch permanently etched into our minds, and we became focused on making it a reality.

The next huge milestone was informing our parents of our crazy, hare-brained plan to marry. I turned 17 the previous December, but Vangie was still only 16, as her birthday is July 29th.

As Vangie continuously mulled everything over in her mind, she began to carefully plan the details of our entire marriage process. She felt it was wise to wait until after her 17th birthday to marry. We looked at a calendar and determined that August 17th would be perfect.

We also determined that we would sell my GTO and use the money from the sale to buy furniture, a bed, and other necessary items to start married life together. We would use her Datsun as our primary vehicle, and if needed, we could buy an inexpensive second vehicle.

I realized that besides being beautiful, she was a practical, down-to-earth, sensible thinker. I tend to make decisions or develop a spur of the moment plan, and then walk directly where angels fear to tread. Not Vangie. She started working out details I had not even considered. She did not want a big wedding. She would use her older sister, Gloria's, wedding dress to save money. We were doing this quickly, sensibly, and for a minimum of cost. After all, according to Vangie, a wedding is just an expensive party.

We knew we must have a good plan and our ducks in a row when we announced to our parents that we were marrying. After all, someone had to sign for her to get married because she was under 18 years old.

We told her folks first. We felt they would be easier than telling mine. That was an understatement. Vangie made sure I understood that her dad, Alex, was very old- fashioned and that it was essential that I ask for her hand in marriage from him first.

Alex was still an imposing figure to me, but in the several weeks we had been together, much of our time was spent at her house. I had gotten to know Alex well and liked him. He was far more laid-back than I originallythought.

Vangie arranged for him and I to be alone at their house to request his daughter's hand in marriage. I was far more nervous than I thought, but I knew I had to do this.

After arriving at their house, Vangie told her mom she wanted to show her something out front. They exited the front door, and I sat down in a plush chair facing her dad, who was sitting on the couch.

"Alex, I would like your permission to marry yourdaughter." I didn't make small talk. I decided to jump in and get it over with.

"Which one?" Alex asked wryly with a mischievous smile. I laughed. Even though he had only an eighth-grade education, he was a very intelligent man. He was the oldest of 8 or 9 kids and quit school to help support his family.

I decided that two could play his game. "Which one do you want to get rid of the most?"

Without any apparent thought, he replied, "Not Vangie. She is my favorite." His demeanor turned more serious now. He wasn't entirely kidding. It was well known in the Aguilar home that Vangie was and always had been his favorite.

Whoops. It seemed my plan to be humorous backfired on me. I decided I must move the conversation forward. I jumped right into sales mode.

"We have thought it over and feel we can make things work financially."

"I am not worried about the financial side near as muchas I am that you both finish high school." His voice took onan even more serious tone. "If I give you my blessing, will you both finish high school?"

"Absolutely!" I replied enthusiastically. "Vangie only needs a few credits to graduate, and I know the importance of a high school diploma. We WILL graduate!" I put extra emphasis on the "will" graduate part.

Alex looked at me for a moment. "You have my blessing." I relaxed and let out a big sigh. This went better than I had expected.

Vangie and her mom returned a bit later, and we told them the news. Cordie gave me a big hug. She liked me. I liked her. I felt she would be a good mother-in-law.

That evening, I stayed at their house for a couple of hours to discuss our wedding plans. I already felt wholly accepted into their family. My folks, I knew, would be a completely different story. We asked Alex and Cordie to hold the wedding information until I talked to my parents. Iknew this would not go well.

The next day I told my folks I had to talk to them about something important. This immediately got their hackles up because I was normally not a cryptic person. When I asked them to sit down together, the tension in the room almost squeezed the oxygen out.

"Mom, Dad," I spoke slowly and emotionless, "Vangie and I have decided to get married." The words barely cleared my lips when Mom gasped, dropped her head, and turned ashen. Dad's eyes widened manically and he immediately erupted.

"Of all the ridiculous things I have ever heard, it is this!" He exclaimed with a jutted jaw, and the veins on his forehead popping out. His eyes were crazy-mad. "You haven't even finished high school. How long have you even known this girl?" Not waiting for an answer, his voice jumped an octave. "This is total, complete, horse shit." He then stood up and bolted straight out of the room, violently shaking his head while mumbling something unrepeatable under his breath.

Mom just slumped in the chair, looking sick to her stomach. I wasn't sure whether I should leave or wait for her to say something. She had a look of hopelessness in her eyes. I felt bad because Dad had always been hard on her, and she had years of minimal joy catering to him and six lazy kids. She waited on us hand and foot our whole lives. Few people knew to what extent we made her our household servant.

We would all be sitting at the dinner table eating a meal, and any one of us could ask for a drink of water, and she would immediately jump up and fetch us a glass of water or whatever we requested. None of us ever made our beds… She did. None of us ever picked up our dirty clothes… She did. None of us ever washed or ironed… She did. None of us lifted a finger to clean anything in the house… She did. Plus, she worked full-time at the Morgan Elementary School Hot Lunch program. This woman was a true beast of burden and a human dynamo. She never slowed down while continuously waiting on others.

"You know, Mark." She started talking slowly, wistfully. "In every marriage, there is a giver and a taker. If you are the taker, it gets old fast." She paused and her voice trailed-off before quietly repeating. "I mean, really fast."

"It's not like that, Mom. Vangie and I are close and get along really well." I felt terrible for her right now. I wanted desperately to say something that would comfort her.

"If you two are truly in love, why couldn't you wait a year to be married?" She looked at me pleadingly. "If it is a good thing now, it would be a good thing then, if it is meant to be." I couldn't answer because I really didn't have a *good* answer. While I was thinking about what she had just said, Dad called out angrily from the other room.

"Mark, get in here. I want to talk to you!" Judging by his voice, he was still crazy mad. He immediately launched into an expletive-driven diatribe. "I don't have a clue what is happening in that damn pea-brain of yours, but I'll tell you what I will do." He softened his voice and gave me an odd, crazy-eyed smile. "I will buy you a brand-new car and send you to Tijuana with enough money to get 'it' out of your system." He looked at me to ensure I knew what he was referring to about getting 'it' out of my system. "You just walk away from this ridiculously stupid idea." Before I could even answer, he continued. "By God, you WILL finish high school, do you hear me?"

"We are finishing school, Dad."

He dropped his voice, looked me straight in the eye and spit the next words out in an angry, staccato rhythm. "Do me one favor, you think this over for at least a few months.

You register for your senior year and finish it, then if you still think you want to get married, we will talk then."

I knew I should leave. Nothing would lighten the mood or sway them to my side. However, the weirdest thing happened. Something overcame me, and I blurted loudly, "Dear God, please help me here…" It just, literally, flew out of my mouth like I was remotely controlled, and was listening to someone speaking through me. It shocked me. It shocked him. We just stared at each other for a moment.

I immediately turned and walked out of the house, somewhat numb and marveling at what had just blasted from my oral cavity. I expected him to come after me or even try and hit me. He never said a word. He never followed me. I just got in the GTO and, burning my tires, sped away from the house. I drove around for an   hour before stopping at Vangie's house. It didn't matter what he thought. Things were irreversibly in motion now.

~**6**~

THE WEDDING AND THE GOVERNOR

The week of July 22ND, 1974 was the annual Deltarado Days celebration. The festival began in Delta as a week- long event in 1920 called the "Annual Farmers Spree." In 1936, the Delta Chamber of Commerce held a "name the event" contest, won by Mrs. Glen Ellington, the postmaster's wife, who suggested "Deltarado Days," earning a $15 prize. Humble beginnings should never be despised. This festival evolved into a major annual spectacle for this small western Colorado farming community.

Deltarado Days grew into a grand, multi-day celebration featuring parades, rodeos, barbecues, dances, and every form of outdoor entertainment imaginable. By 1974, races were a significant part of the festivities. Colorado Governor John Vanderhoof and Carl Akers, the legendary Channel 9 news anchor from Denver, were both present as trophy presenters at the races that night.

One of the highlights was the Australian Pursuit race, where the winner received a handshake from the Governor and Carl Akers, along with a large trophy cup filled with 75 silver dollars—a considerable sum in 1974.

Although the Australian Pursuit was the main event, the night also featured a demolition derby and other crazy activities. With such grand proceedings, it was undoubtably the most celebrated night in the racetrack's history. The parking lot on the hill was full, with people parking along the highway leading to the track. Local farmers transported people in the backs of their pickup trucks up the incline to find a viewing spot on the hill.

This was the largest gathering of stock cars and spectators ever assembled at the track. Racers, drawn by the substantial cash prizes for the top three finishers, were eager to compete. The pits were crowded and chaotic, with alcohol, despite the "NO ALCOHOLIC BEVERAGES IN THE PITS" signs, being prevalent. The engine noise, deafening on a normal race night, was beyond pandemonium that night.

I performed well in the first two races, finishing third in the heat race. I didn't give much thought to the Australian Pursuit because it was clear that some incredibly fast cars and talented drivers were competing for the large silver cupcontaining 75 silver dollars plus over $200 in additional cash.

An Australian Pursuit is a peculiar race where if you arepassed, you are eliminated and must exit the track into the pits. The last car remaining on the track wins. Frankly, whomever designed this race format was an idiot. It eliminates most the thrilling aspects of dirt track racing where drivers jockey for position. In this race, if you were passed, you were eliminated and simply left the track.

Due to the number of cars, the racetrack was at capacity. When the green flag dropped, every racer accelerated, eliminating half the field in the first few laps. Remarkably, Dwayne McCarty, with his fearsome lime green Mopar and large wing, got wedged between two other cars, allowing me to easily pass him. He was eliminated early in the race.

I still clearly remember passing him and briefly making eye contact. His look of disbelief was memorable. To this day, I can't understand how it happened so quickly. It was pure luck rather than skill or a faster car that led to my victory in the Australian Pursuit. It was simply being in the right place at the right time.

Before I knew it, I was shaking Governor John Vanderhoof's hand and receiving the trophy cup filled with silver dollars. After the presentation, I left the pits, crossed the track, carried the cup up the hill, and presented it to… *Vangie*. This heightened the already unbearable tension between Dad and me.

The next day, the front page of the Delta County Independent featured a large picture of me receiving the trophy from the Governor with the caption, "Mark Gregg receives congratulations and upcoming wedding wishes from the Governor." Many years later, I discovered Dad had clipped the article and saved it in his personal papers. I was surprised; maybe he wasn't as disappointed as he let on.

From then until the wedding on August 17th, Vangie and I spent as much time together as possible. Although we lived in Montrose, Vangie found a ring she liked at a small jewelry store on Main Street in Delta. We bought it with some cash from selling my GTO and the track winnings from Deltarado Days. It wasn't expensive, but it was pretty and looked good on her dainty hand.

Angered by our impending marriage, Dad stopped working on the stock car. I managed to keep it running, often working on it at the track. Vangie and I enjoyedracing and frequently worked on it together.

The final weeks before the wedding were busy and hectic. We attended a couple of auctions to buy used furniture and a bed. We rented a single-bedroom apartment at the new Park Garden Apartments, built on the dirt hills where I used to ride bicycles with friends.

We moved our "quality pre-owned" furniture, a new stereo system, and a 19" TV (a must) into the apartment a few days before the wedding. Cordie gave us most of our dishes, silverware, and kitchen utensils so we could return from the honeymoon and immediately "*play house*," as Dad sarcastically called it.

We didn't send formal invitations to the wedding. We didn't care who came or if anyone came at all. We wanted a simple, low-budget event. We did hire a photographer, and I'm glad we did. The family photos captured the comical disgust and disapproval of my family over the wedding. Dad was vocal in his disdain and gave us, at most, six months before the marriage would fall apart. In all the wedding pictures, his arms were crossed, and his expression was one of frustration or anger. Mom looked distant, as though she were at a funeral rather than a wedding, and there were tears on her cheeks that seemed more sorrowful than joyful.

Despite the lack of formal invitations, the First Christian Church in Montrose was at maximum capacity. We later thought this was due to speculation that Vangie might be pregnant. In 1974, premarital sex was a subject of gossip. However, Vangie was not pregnant. We had not been intimate. Despite my efforts, Vangie remained steadfast in her commitment to purity. To this day, she exemplifies true integrity and character.

My brother Larry was the best man. He was married to an attractive blonde named Melody, and they had a two- year-old son named Shawn. Known for his small size, quickness, and smart-aleck attitude, he had a few previous encounters with the local police and was notorious for his fighting prowess. His poor relationship with Dad, due to their similar personalities, never allowed for any harmony between them.

Our wedding day was swift and eventful. Mom and Cordie couldn't stand each other, though they laterreconciled and became friends. The wedding was, at best, a disaster. Mom warned Pastor Lloyd McMillan that she intended to protest our marriage during the ceremony. Lloyd skipped the part where he normally said, *"If any of you can show just cause why they may not be lawfully wed, speak now, or else forever hold your peace"*. This was to avoid a huge, embarrassing issue. Immediately after the ceremony, Mom and Cordie had a significant argument thatalmost required physical separation.

The climax of the tense wedding day was the arrival of an ambulance to the church. Alex slipped and hurt his injured leg in the parking lot. The EMTs took him to the hospital for a brief visit. I think he was mourning the marriage of his favorite daughter to me. Despite the difficulties, Alex always treated me like a son, and I have deep respect for him for that along with many other reasons.

Vangie and I made our appearance at the reception, sharing a piece of wedding cake and our first toast as a married couple. I was eager to change out of my wedding clothes and head to Durango, where a Ramada Inn hotel room awaited us. Being seventeen years old, my primary focus was on the physical aspects of the honeymoon. In retrospect, I regret not appreciating it for more than just the physical moments. The concept of two individuals becoming one, both physically and spiritually, is a profound aspect of marriage.

In my later years of teaching electrical theory, I compare marriage to a bar magnet. Two separate magnets have distinct magnetic flux lines. When combined, they form one magnet with a unified set of flux lines. This is similar to marriage, where two people become one.

I provided extensive marriage counseling to coworkers and others in later years and believe that selfishness is the root cause of most divorces. Whether it is adultery, sickness, financial issues, or abuse, selfishness is often at the core.

If you reflect deeply on train wrecks in marriages, you can trace them back to selfishness by one or both partners. Ideally, two people should become one, which should eliminate selfishness. When it doesn't, marriages fall apart.

The honeymoon was just a two-day affair in Durango because we needed to return and register for our senior year at Montrose High School. Clearly, our lives were quite different from those of typical high school seniors. We moved into our small apartment and could miss school whenever we wanted. We crafted our own excuses for absences. The exact wording didn't matter. *We were adults now* and decided when it was appropriate to skip school. This frustration was evident to the secretaries in the attendance office at Montrose High School, as we regularly missed classes.

Unfortunately, about halfway through our senior year, I was informed that I didn't have enough credits to graduate. What? WHAT? Despite my hard work, academic success, and consistently responsible behavior throughout high school, I found out I was short on credits. Who could have predicted this? Certainly not me (obviously).

Honestly, years of freeloading and irresponsibility caught up with me. I couldn't graduate with my class in 1975 due to insufficient credits. This was a huge blow. My options were straightforward: return in 1976 to earn the necessary credits or quit school—tough choice. I took the easy route… I quit school. Not surprisingly, given my track record of irresponsibility, I was, at least, consistent.

Vangie chose to quit at the same time I did. The difference was that she only needed a few credits to graduate. We decided to focus full-time on our jobs and make more money rather than "waste" time at Montrose High School. Scientists say a teenager's brain doesn't fully mature until their early to mid-20s. I can confidently confirm this is true.

My entire goal in life was now to get hired at a power plant. I couldn't believe that quitting school wouldjeopardize this. At least, I hoped it wouldn't.

THE WURLITZER ORGAN COMPANY CEO

The next 18 months were a whirlwind of work, racing, drinking, new jobs, and moving. We decided we didn't like Park Garden Apartments and relocated to the country into a two-room apartment on a working farm called Kris Estates—a major mistake. The walls of this cheaply built tenement were paper-thin. You could hear EVERYTHING happening in the adjoining apartment. To make matters worse, we had a wife-beater in the adjacent unit. Field mice claimed ownership of the entire complex, running freely and unchecked in the halls, bedrooms, cabinets, furniture, and anywhere else they pleased. We quickly grew tired of Kris Estates and decided we wanted a house, not an apartment.

We moved to 344 West Main Street in Montrose. This was a small two-bedroom house built in the 1920s that had been hastily cleaned and converted into a rental property. The landlord was an old pervert who seemed to revolve his life around talking about sex. At least, that was my impression. He lived next door in a similar house with his latest wife. Our house was painted avocado green and was, by all accounts, a total dump. Nevertheless, we were glad to be away from the apartment scene.

I began sending resumes to various power companies in Colorado and the surrounding states. I didn't care where we went so long as it was to work in a power plant. A few years earlier, Larry had been hired by Colorado Ute

Electric Association as an operator at their power plant in Hayden, Colorado. We had visited him once, and I was absolutely determined to get a job at one of these plants. Their size and mechanical complexity fascinated me.

I checked the mail daily, but it was always filled with bills. No power company seemed interested in a high school dropout from Montrose, Colorado. *Who knew?*

Our lives settled into a repetitive cycle of work, pizza, and beer. We dined out constantly, mostly at fast food places, and often paired our pizza with a pitcher or two of beer. If we weren't having pizza, we'd still eat out and then head to Pizza Hut or Pizza Inn for a pitcher of beer. Beer became the common denominator in our routine—lots of beer.

Vangie wasn't a big drinker. She would nurse one mug of beer all evening and be content. I wasn't content until I felt no pain. For those who don't know what this means, it simply meant I drank a ton of beer… All the time.

Occasionally, I'd have some wine. Not the "sniff the bouquet, swirl the enticing liquid while inspecting the color and coating on the glass" kind of wine. I'm talking Boone's Farm Apple Adventure or Peach Pleasure. We're talking Mogen David 20/20 Grape Wine, commonly known as Mad Dog 20/20. It wasn't about taste; it was entirely about the alcohol.

As time went on, I found myself drinking a pitcher of beer, getting hammered, and then going to the restroom. I'd stand at the urinal and say a little prayer, asking God to forgive me for drinking so much. This became a routine. I would drink, go to the bathroom, and ask for forgiveness for drinking so much. Sadly, I didn't ask for help to stop drinking; I just asked for forgiveness for drinking so much. With 20/20 hindsight, it's clear that I should have asked for help to drink less. Remember, the teenage brain doesn't mature until the mid-20s.

Vangie often joined me in the garage to work on cars. She was quite proficient with tools and car engines and was exceptionally mechanically inclined.

One rainy Saturday afternoon, as we were about to close the shop and rush to Pizza Inn for pizza and beer, a large motorhome pulled into the station. A gentleman, who was probably in his late 40s (extremely old to us at that time), got out of the motorhome and entered the office. I was lamenting that I didn't lock the office door sooner. I just wanted to end the day with a beer.

As this gentleman approached the office, I marveled at how classy and sophisticated he looked. He was fit, well- groomed, and wearing a tailor-fit, monogrammed golf shirt paired with dress slacks sporting razor-sharp pleats.

"Excuse me, young man, I was wondering if you could help me?" His deep, gentle voice and air of confidence reminded me of an actor. He stood tall and straight with his head held high. "My motorhome's power steering has stopped working, and I need to get it fixed before Monday if at all possible." I sensed urgency in his voice.

We both knew that 5:30 P.M. on a Saturday was a terrible time to need repairs, especially in a small western Colorado town of less than 10,000 people. It had been raining sporadically all day, and I certainly didn't feel like working into the evening. However, I noticed a woman and a few children staring at us from inside the motorhome's panoramic front glass. I considered it for a moment and decided I should at least take a quick look to see what might be wrong with the power steering on his large rig.

The motorhome wouldn't fit into the filling station garage, so I had to crawl under it on the wet concrete in front of the shop. It quickly became apparent that a hydraulic hose for the power steering system had blown, covering the bottom of the motorhome with hot, dark-red hydraulic fluid. It was dripping everywhere, including on me. The auto parts store closed at 6:00 P.M., and it was already 5:45. While I was under the front end peering at the maze of hoses dripping with crimson fluid, his wife and kids entered the office.

After discovering the ruptured hose, I crawled out from under the motorhome and returned to the office to give them the bad news. Vangie was talking with the family, who were as well-dressed and groomed as he was. From their laughter and smiles, it seemed they enjoyed Vangie's company, and she enjoyed theirs.

I quickly called the auto parts store and confirmed they had a generic hose kit that would work. I had to move fast to get to the parts store before it closed. I felt strangely comfortable leaving Vangie alone with this family. I drove quickly to the store and bought the hose kit. When I returned to the garage, another rain squall was brewing on the valley floor.

Changing the hose left me drenched almost head-to-toe in painfully hot, stinky hydraulic oil. There wasn't a patch of my skin or clothes that wasn't soaked with this malodorous red mess. The hydraulic fluid left me smelling like pungent burned rubber combined with strong body sweat when I returned to the office. I was still greeted warmly by the distinguished gentleman.

"I appreciate your efforts, young man," he said gratefully, his eyes scanning me from head to toe. "I would have undoubtedly been stuck here until Monday if not for you and your wonderful wife." I acknowledged this while wiping grease and power steering fluid from my hair and face.

He then looked at me inquisitively and quietly asked, "What do you want out of life, young man?" His sincerity seemed genuine. A quick shiver ran down my back as his eyes narrowed and he focused directly on my response. His stare and gentle nature instilled a feeling of peace deep inside my heart.

"I want to work in a power plant. It's all I've wanted for as long as I can remember. The problem is, they're difficult to get into because a lot of people want these jobs." He glanced at his wife, who returned a mutual look. Vangie and I were too young at the time to understand how a long-time married couple could communicate with a mere glance.

"Well, young man, I don't have any connections in the utility industry, but my wife and I will certainly pray that you get that job." I was shocked at his response. I don't think anyone had ever told me they'd pray for me outside of church. He reached into his rear hip pocket, retrieved his wallet, and handed me a business card. It read:

William Hurlemann President, Wurlitzer Organ Company

I was taken aback when he handed me his business card. He was the president of a large multinational corporation, and as we stood there in the office, he calmly told me he'd pray for me. Hearing someone so influential say that with such conviction was almost surreal. He didn't just offer words of encouragement—he promised I'd get the job at the power plant I'd been desperately waiting for.

Standing before this man, whose name was known in circles far beyond my own, I felt something shift. Alongside Governor John Vanderhoof and Carl Akers from Channel 9 News in Denver, he was among the most notable people I'd ever crossed paths with. Yet, here he was, casually talking to me about prayer as if he had a direct line to God.

He told me that he and his wife were devout Christians who prayed together regularly. "I am certain you will hear from a power plant," he said, his voice filled with certainty. There was no doubt in him—only a quiet confidence that felt prophetic.

After a few more words, he paid his bill, and they climbed into their massive motorhome. I watched them disappear down Townsend Avenue, his business card still in my hand, wondering if I'd just met a man with a gift, or if I was merely swept up in the moment.

I never saw him again, but I held on to that business card for many years, reflecting occasionally on his strange, yet comforting words. They lingered with me, like a whispered promise that wouldn't fade.

That evening, Vangie and I closed the shop, went home, and tried to shake off the day with pizza and beer. But his words remained with me.

A few months later, when the phone finally rang, it wasn't just another call—it was *the* call. The one I had been waiting for. But what made it even more extraordinary was the timing—it came when everything was hanging by a thread... At the precise moment when I needed it the most.

What happened next was nothing short of life- altering—far beyond anything I could have imagined. But that's a story for another time, one I wasn't prepared for, one that I didn't see coming…